DISCAR

OUTDATED, REDUNDANT
MATERIAL.

D1200337

Date: 1/19/16

BR 796.962 LIN
Lindeen, Mary.
Let's play hockey /

PALM BEACH COUNTY
LIBRARY SYSTEM
3650 SUMMIT BLVD.
WEST PALM BEACH, FL 33406

A Beginning-to-Read Book

Let's Play Hockey

by Mary Lindeen

NORWOOD HOUSE PRESS

DEAR CAREGIVER, The *Beginning to Read—Read and Discover* books provide emergent readers the opportunity to explore the world through nonfiction while building early reading skills. The text integrates both common sight words and content vocabulary. These key words are featured on lists provided at the back of the book to help your child expand his or her sight word recognition, which helps build reading fluency. The content words expand vocabulary and support comprehension.

Nonfiction text is any text that is factual. The Common Core State Standards call for an increase in the amount of informational text reading among students. The Standards aim to promote college and career readiness among students. Preparation for college and career endeavors requires proficiency in reading complex informational texts in a variety of content areas. You can help your child build a foundation by introducing nonfiction early. To further support the CCSS, you will find Reading Reinforcement activities at the back of the book that are aligned to these Standards.

Above all, the most important part of the reading experience is to have fun and enjoy it!

Sincerely,

Shannon Cannon

Shannon Cannon, Ph.D.
Literacy Consultant

Norwood House Press • P.O. Box 316598 • Chicago, Illinois 60631
For more information about Norwood House Press please visit our website at
www.norwoodhousepress.com or call 866-565-2900.
© 2016 Norwood House Press. Beginning-to-Read™ is a trademark of Norwood House Press.
All rights reserved. No part of this book may be reproduced or utilized in any form or by any
means without written permission from the publisher.

Editor: Judy Kentor Schmauss
Designer: Lindaanne Donohoe

Photo Credits:

Shutterstock, cover, 1, 3 (Pavel L Photo and Video), 4-5 (Paolo Bona), 6 (Ivica Drusany), 7 (Herbert Kratky), 8-9 (Mitrofanov Alexander), 12-13 (Paolo Bona), 14 (Iurii Osadchi), 15 (Pukhov Konstantin), 16-17 (Iurii Osadchi), 18-19 (Herbert Kratky), 20-21 (Lazlo Szirtesi), 22-23 (Iurii Osadchi), 24-25 (Arina P Habich), 28-29 (Iurii Osadchi); Dreamstime, 10-11 (©lofoto), 26-27 (©Embe2006)

Library of Congress Cataloging-in-Publication Data
Lindeen, Mary.
  Let's play hockey / by Mary Lindeen.
     pages cm. – (A Beginning to Read Book)
  Summary: "Hockey is a team sport that is played on ice. Players wear skates, helmets, and pads.
  They use hockey sticks to get the puck into the other team's net. Find out about the coach, referees,
  and how to win a game. This title includes reading activities and a word list"– Provided by publisher.
  Audience: Grade: K to Grade 3.
  ISBN 978-1-59953-686-6 (Library Edition : alk. paper)
  ISBN 978-1-60357-771-7 (eBook)
  1. Hockey-Juvenile literature. I. Title. II. Title: Let us play hockey.
  GV847.25.L47 2015
  796.356-dc23
                                            2014047625

Manufactured in the United States of America in Stevens Point, Wisconsin. 275N-062015

Hockey is a team sport.
You play it on ice.

Hockey players wear skates with long blades.

They go fast!

Players can fall.

They can bump into each other.

Players wear pads and helmets.

These help keep the players safe.

Each team has
a coach.

The coach helps
them play better.

Two teams play each other.

Each team can have six players on the ice.

Each player has a hockey stick.

Players use their sticks
to push a puck.

The puck slides on the ice.

Players try to make a goal.

They try to get the puck into the other team's net.

This player is the goalie.

She tries to keep the puck out of the net.

This player did it.

He made a goal.

His team gets one
point.

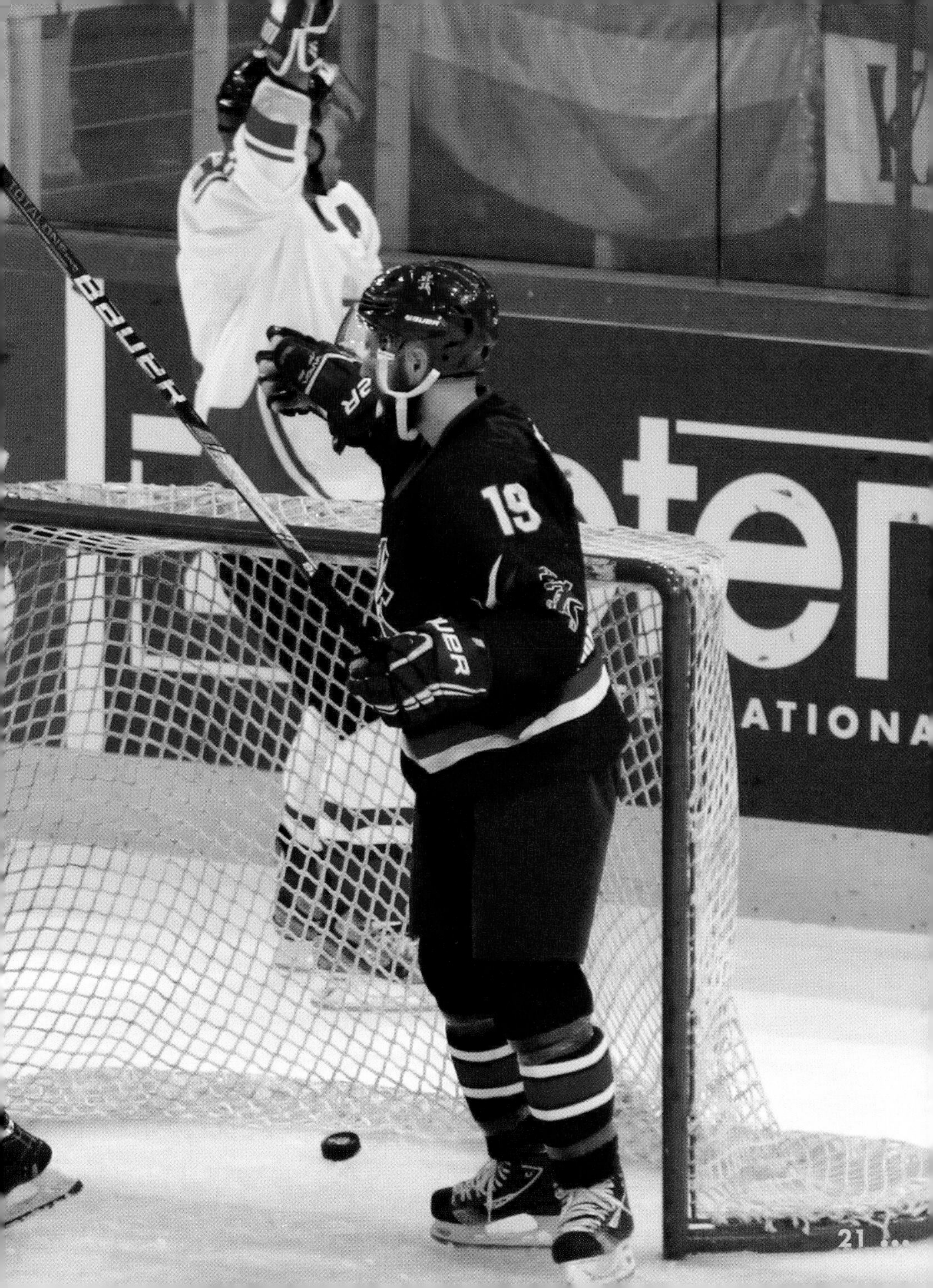
BAUER
19
ATIONA

Each game also has referees.

They make sure everyone follows the rules.

You can play hockey outside.

It can be a small game.

You can play
hockey inside.

It can be a big
game.

This team won the game.

Good job!

...READING REINFORCEMENT...

CRAFT AND STRUCTURE

To check your child's understanding of this book, recreate the following diagram on a sheet of paper. Read the book with your child, then help him or her fill in the diagram using what they learned. Work together to complete the diagram by using the word in each square as a prompt for writing questions and answers about hockey.

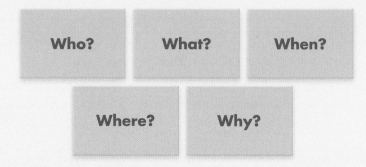

Who? What? When?

Where? Why?

VOCABULARY: Learning Content Words

Content words are words that are specific to a particular topic. All of the content words for this book can be found on page 32. Use some or all of these content words to complete one or more of the following activities:

- Say a content word and have your child act out its meaning.

- Write each word and each definition on separate cards. Play a memory game by turning all cards face down and then turning them over to find matching pairs of words and definitions.

- As you write a content word, scramble the order of the letters. Give your child a definition of the word. Have him or her use the definition and the letters to guess the word. Ask him or her to unscramble the letters to spell the word correctly.

- Write the content words on slips of paper. Place them in a box. Have your child pick a word and use it in a sentence.

- Help your child look for a smaller word within each content word. Make a list of the content words that have smaller words within them.

FOUNDATIONAL SKILLS: Consonant digraphs

Consonant digraphs are two consonants that together make a single sound (for example, *ph* in *phone*). Have your child identify the consonant digraphs in the list below. Then help your child find the words with consonant digraphs in this book.

coach	hockey	skates
fall	puck	sticks
ice	push	safe

CLOSE READING OF INFORMATIONAL TEXT

Close reading helps children comprehend text. It includes reading a text, discussing it with others, and answering questions about it. Use these questions to discuss this book with your child:

- What are three true things about hockey?

- What is the difference between your shoes and ice skates?

- What questions would you ask a hockey goalie?

- How is a puck similar to a soccer ball?

- What suggestions would you have for helping a hockey team whose ice rink is melting?

- What do you think about hockey?

FLUENCY

Fluency is the ability to read accurately with speed and expression. Help your child practice fluency by using one or more of the following activities:

- Reread this book to your child at least two times while he or she uses a finger to track each word as you read it.

- Read the first sentence aloud. Then have your child reread the sentence with you. Continue until you have finished this book.

- Ask your child to read aloud the words they know on each page of this book. (Your child will learn additional words with subsequent readings.)

- Have your child practice reading this book several times to improve accuracy, rate, and expression.

••• Word List •••

Let's Play Hockey uses the 79 words listed below. *High-frequency* words are those words that are used most often in the English language. They are sometimes referred to as sight words because children need to learn to recognize them automatically when they read. *Content words* are any words specific to a particular topic. Regular practice reading these words will enhance your child's ability to read with greater fluency and comprehension.

High Frequency Words

a	go	it	out	to
also	good	keep	she	two
and	has	long	small	use
be	have	made	the	with
big	he	make	their	you
can	help(s)	of	them	
did	his	on	these	
each	into	one	they	
get(s)	is	other	this	

Content Words

better	game	keep	referees	sure
blades	goal	net	rules	team(s, 's
bump	goalie	outside	safe	tries
coach	helmets	pads	six	try
everyone	hockey	play(er, ers)	skates	wear
fall	ice	point	slides	won
fast	inside	puck	sport	
follows	job	push	stick(s)	

••• About the Author

Mary Lindeen is a writer, editor, parent, and former elementary school teacher. She has written more than 100 books for children and edited many more. She specializes in early literacy instruction and books for young readers, especially nonfiction.

••• About the Advisor

Dr. Shannon Cannon is a teacher educator in the School of Education at UC Davis, where she also earned her Ph.D. in Language, Literacy, and Culture. She serves on the clinical faculty, supervising pre-service teachers and teaching elementary methods courses in reading, effective teaching, and teacher action research.